The Tickets

Written by
Rob Waring and **Maurice Jamall**

Before You Read

to fall

to hit

class

lunch

lunchroom

money

bag

purse

tickets

angry

hungry

late

surprised

In the story

 Jenny

 Jimmy

 Kerry

 Alex

"Happy birthday, Jenny!" says her friend Jimmy. Today is Jenny's birthday.

"These are for you," he says. Jimmy gives Jenny some tickets for her birthday.

"Wow! The tickets are for *The Bandits*. I love them!" Jenny says. "Thank you, Jimmy."

Jimmy says, "There are two tickets. There's one for you and one for Alex."

Alex is Jenny's boyfriend.

Jenny is very happy. Jenny's friend Kerry looks at the tickets.
"Wow!" she says. "When is it?"
Jimmy says, "It's on Saturday."
"Lucky you!" says Kerry. "I want to go!"
"But there are no more tickets," says Jimmy.

"But I really want to go," says Kerry. "Please give me a ticket, Jenny."

"Sorry," says Jenny. "These are *my* tickets. I'm going with Alex."

"Please?" asks Kerry. "I love *The Bandits,* but Alex doesn't like them."

Jenny and Jimmy are very surprised.

"No," says Jimmy. "They're Jenny's tickets. She wants to go with Alex."

Jimmy looks at the time. "Look, Jenny!" he says. "We're late for class."

"Okay, let's go!" says Jenny. "Are you coming, Kerry?"

Kerry says, "No, I don't have class now. See you at lunchtime."

"Bye!" they say.

Jimmy and Jenny go to class. They are really late.

Jimmy and Jenny go to the classroom.
A boy is running to class. He hits Jenny's bag.
"Oh, I'm sorry," he says.
"It's okay," says Jenny.
Something falls from Jenny's bag. Kerry sees it.
Jenny does not see it.
Jenny goes into the classroom.

Kerry sees Jenny's tickets. "What's that?" she thinks. "Wow! These are Jenny's tickets!"
Kerry looks at the tickets, "I want to go, but they are not *my* tickets. They are Jenny's."
"Jenny's in her class now, but we are meeting at lunchtime," she thinks. She puts the tickets in her purse.

In class, Jenny says, "Alex, I want to show you something."
She looks in her bag for the tickets. They are not there.
Jenny says to Jimmy, "Jimmy! The tickets! Where are the
tickets? They're not in my bag!"
"Oh no!" says Jimmy. "Where are they?"

It is lunchtime. Kerry is waiting for Jenny and Jimmy. Jenny's tickets are in Kerry's purse. She wants to give the tickets to Jenny.

Kerry thinks, "Where is Jenny? I have her tickets."

But Jenny does not come.

Jimmy comes to the lunchroom.

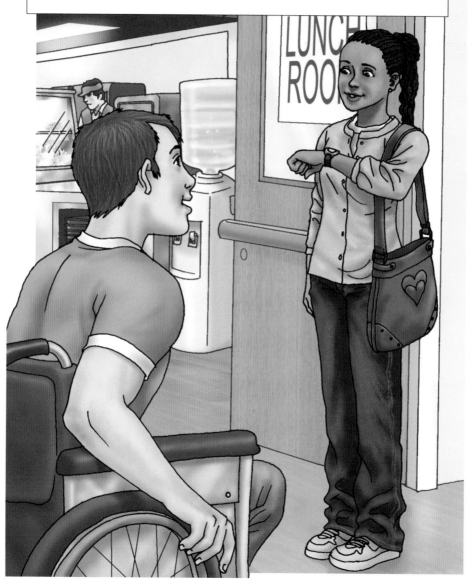

"Hi, Jimmy," says Kerry.
"Hi, let's have lunch. I'm very hungry," says Jimmy.
"Where's Jenny?" asks Kerry. "I have something for her."
Jimmy says, "She's coming, Kerry. Let's eat. I'm really hungry."
"Okay," she says.

Kerry gets a sandwich. She opens her purse. She takes out some money.

Jimmy sees Jenny's tickets in Kerry's purse. He is very surprised. Jimmy thinks, "Why does Kerry have Jenny's tickets?"

He thinks, "Oh, I know! Kerry wants the tickets. She wants to go to the concert. That's really bad!"

Jimmy is angry with Kerry. "Kerry, that's very bad," says Jimmy.
"Excuse me?" says Kerry. She is very surprised.
"Jenny's your friend!" says Jimmy.
"Yes, Jenny's my friend," she says.

Jimmy says, "But you're *not* a good friend!"

Jimmy is thinking about Jenny's tickets. They are in Kerry's purse.

"What are you saying?" says Kerry. "I don't understand."

Jimmy says, "That's really bad of you."

"Jimmy, what are you talking about?" asks Kerry.

Jenny comes into the lunchroom. Kerry and Jimmy
see Jenny.

"Oh! Jenny! Here are your tickets," says Kerry.
Kerry tells Jenny about the tickets.

"Thanks, Kerry," says Jenny. "That's very nice of you."
Jimmy thinks, "Oh no! Kerry *doesn't* want the tickets.
She's a *good* friend."

Jimmy is very surprised. Jenny shows the tickets to Alex.
Kerry asks, "Jimmy, why are you angry with me? I don't
understand."
"I'm sorry. It's okay. It's nothing!" he says.
Kerry looks at Jimmy. "Nothing?"
Jimmy's face is very red. "Yes, nothing."